MW01012008

When the hard days come, it can be so difficult to praise God. from him that we tend to forget how our lives are deper he actually dwells in our praises. With her beautiful images and a heart for the practice of praise, Julie lovingly circles us back to an attitude of praise where the protection and provision of praising God for who he is {no matter how hard the days} lifts us right back to him. Where we need to be."

—**Jo Ann Fore,** author, *When a Woman Finds Her Voice*

"Everyday Praise is a wonderful 30 day devotional that will inspire your heart to praise your Savior, even through difficult circumstances. Julie's writing stems from her own challenging experiences and I found her words to be soothing and uplifting."

—**Rachel Wojnarowski,** author, *One More Step*

"Julie Sunne's book, Everyday Praise, is an inspiring invitation to greater peace. Every carefully crafted message is a spirit-led encouragement that serves as a healing balm for any weary soul. Julie offers compelling narrative and practical application. This devotional is an excellent reminder of God's all-sufficiency for any season."

—**Marisa Shadrick,** blogger and speaker

"If you're looking for a 'life-is-always-great-and-God's-just-wonderful' kind of devotion book, this probably isn't for you. But if you want a tried-in-the-trenches perspective for when life gets hard and God feels distant, Julie Sunne has created a beautiful work that will encourage your heart. With practical insights gleaned from biblical wisdom, you'll also gain "the added bonus of seeing true praise and worship in a whole new light when it comes to surviving the storms of life."

—**Stephanie Raquel,** Devotions Manager, Proverbs 31 Ministries

"In Everyday Praise, Julie Sunne has captured many subtle, yet extremely powerful, messages that can lift our days (and our spirits). Many devotionals can become overwhelming, as they try to pack too much substance into each page. Not this book. Between the beauty of the visuals and the clear, crisp use of scriptures and text, Julie allows us to gain power and peace, through concise, meaningful teachable moments. Like a warm hug and encouraging word given from a personal friend or supportive coach, this book lifts the heart and blesses the spirit, allowing you to feel 'centered' and 'at home' with yourself and the day ahead of you. Don't lag behind in your spiritual walk...but don't rush forward either! Just stay in the moment, in peace, present in today and all it offers you. EveryDay Praise will help you do just that. Lovely."

—**Mark Nation,** Global Leadership Executive & Coach. Founder & CEO, Nation Leadership

"Sharing from her own life, author Julie Sunne greatly encourages readers with *Everyday Praise*. Life can get messy, but this book focuses on practicing praise as a vital step we should all take to meet and walk through our messes. With photos, Scriptures, devotionals, reflective questions, and prayers, Julie reminds readers that God is always good, always love, and always near. He deserves our praise, and we *need* to praise Him!"

—**Lisa Parnell,** Friend and Publishing Professional

EVERYDAY

Praise

Walking in Greater Peace

JULIE SUNNE

Copyright © 2016 Julie Sunne
All rights reserved.
ISBN 978-1-5393-2845-2

Scripture quotations marked HCSB®, are taken from the Holman Christian Standard Bible®, Copyright © 1999, 2000, 2002, 2003, 2009 by Holman Bible Publishers. Used by permission. HCSB® is a federally registered trademark of Holman Bible Publishers.

Scripture quotations marked (NIV) are taken from the Holy Bible, New International Version®, NIV®. Copyright © 1973, 1978, 1984, 2011 by Biblica, Inc.™ Used by permission of Zondervan. All rights reserved worldwide. www.zondervan.com The "NIV" and "New International Version" are trademarks registered in the United States Patent and Trademark Office by Biblica, Inc.™

Scripture quotations taken from the New American Standard Bible® (NASB),
Copyright © 1960, 1962, 1963, 1968, 1971, 1972, 1973,
1975, 1977, 1995 by The Lockman Foundation
Used by permission. www.Lockman.org

Scripture quotations marked (ESV) are from the ESV® Bible (The Holy Bible, English Standard Version®), Copyright © 2001 by Crossway, a publishing ministry of Good News Publishers. Used by permission. All rights reserved.

Scripture quotations marked NLT are taken from the Holy Bible, New Living Translation, Copyright © 1996, 2004. Used by permission of Tyndale House Publishers, Inc., Wheaton, Illinois 60189. All rights reserved.

Original photos courtesy of Julie Sunne, Pixabay.com, and Freelyphotos.com.
Scripture images created by Julie Sunne.

To my parents, who showered me with unconditional love, taught me the benefits of perseverance and hard work, and raised me to honor and revere the Lord.

And

To my mother-in-law and late father-in-law, who invited me in as one of their own and have guided me in the finer points of loving Jesus.

Table of Contents

Introduction

I don't have to tell you the world in which we live holds difficult terrain to navigate. You've likely already fallen into a few mud holes, waded flooded streams, or stumbled over rocky riverbanks. Maybe you're in the middle of a desert right now.

Each of us can expect difficulties. Jesus promises: "In this world you will have trouble" (John 16:33b, NIV). Trials then should not take us by surprise. But what do we do when they come?

We should praise God. Yes, you read that right! As counterintuitive as it seems, praising God is the perfect response in any circumstance.

Why Develop the Practice of Praise?

Praising God is the way over any mountain, through any swamp, and across any valley.

When we reflect on the goodness of the Lord, it brings our daily challenges into perspective. No longer do they seem so overwhelming. His power and majesty assure us He can handle all those troubles. In fact, Jesus comforts us later in the same verse: "I have overcome the world."

Despite the trials of this life … in the midst of the hardships, in the ugliness of this world … the Lord is worthy of our praise. And it is to our benefit to do just that.

It took me years of walking with God to realize the great blessing of praising Him. Spending time in prayer and in His Word has fueled a desire to praise Him in all situations! Now through His grace, it's becoming my default.

As I proclaim His praises, my messy life loses its potency. I no longer become paralyzed in unexpected and unwanted circumstances. I see the possibility of peace and joy in the midst of life's storms. I sense God's hand in situations where previously I had felt alone.

You can tap into that same wellspring of peace and joy. As you read, reflect, pray, and praise your way through this little book, may you experience "the length and width, height and depth of God's love" (Ephesians 3:18b, HCSB), right in the thick of your mess.

Peace will follow your heartfelt practice of praise. However, the most compelling reason for everyday praise and worship is that the Lord is worthy! His majesty, power, compassion, and faithfulness claim the highest honor. It's our privilege to give Him the glory He is due.

How To Use This Devotional

Everyday Praise consists of 31 stand-alone devotions. They can be read at whatever timeline is comfortable for you.

Each entry consists of a corresponding full-color Scripture image, a "point to remember" that can be easily memorized, a short text devotion, a reflection section with questions and calls to action, and a short prayer. Although I wrote each devotion to be read quickly and understood easily, I'd encourage you to leave plenty of time to dig into the reflections and let God speak into your heart.

Now as you begin (or hone) the practice of praise, may the God who is ever worthy bless your walk into His greater peace.

"Doth not all nature around me praise God? If I were silent, I should be an exception to the universe. Doth not the thunder praise Him as it rolls like drums in the march of the God of armies? Do not the mountains praise Him when the woods upon their summits wave in adoration? Doth not the lightning write His name in letters of fire? Hath not the whole earth a voice? And shall I, can I, silent be?"

—Charles Spurgeon

Then We Say, "Amen and Praise the Lord!"

"Praise be to the LORD, the God of Israel, from everlasting to everlasting.
Then all the people said 'Amen' and 'Praise the LORD.'"
1 Chronicles 16:36 NIV

The night before the tests, I lay in bed, wondering if tomorrow would bring blessed relief or start a potentially long road of suffering. As I turned over the possibilities, words of the Doxology[1] leaped unbidden to mind, followed immediately by the refrain to "It Is Well With My Soul."[2] Peace enveloped me. I fell into a restful sleep knowing no matter what verdict I heard the next day, all would be well. My physical body may not be, but my spirit would.

I doubt I would have felt the calm assurance 5 years ago that I did that night. The daily practice of praising God has settled my soul. It has reminded me of the steadfast love of my Father. When the unimaginable

Praise settles souls and ushers in lasting peace.

happens, instead of dwelling on the what-ifs, I've equipped myself to remember the promises and faithfulness of my unfathomable God. I let praise usher in lasting peace.

You, too, can develop a habit of everyday praise no matter how dire your circumstances may be. It simply takes some intentionality. Singing the Doxology is a great way to begin.

"Praise God, from Whom all blessings flow;
Praise Him, all creatures here below;
Praise Him above, ye heavenly host;
Praise Father, Son, and Holy Ghost." Thomas Ken, 1674.

Reflections: What elements of praise do you incorporate every day? Song? Prayer? List up to 10 hymns and prayers you can remember (look up some if you need to). Commit to memorizing at least one over the next week.

Dear Father of all Heaven and Earth, nothing is unimaginable to You. You know my circumstances and You know how unsettled I feel at times. But in You, Lord, lies my peace. Help me to tap into that peace by remembering Your goodness and faithfulness. Help me to establish a daily practice of praising You. For You are worthy, and I am needy. In Jesus' name, Amen.

Sing to Him; sing praise to Him; tell about all His wonderful works!

1 Chronicles 16:9

What It Means to Live as a Song of Worship

"Sing to Him; sing praise to Him; tell about all His wonderful works!"
1 Chronicles 16:9 HCSB

Life on this earth isn't all roses. It actually involves a lot of thorns. They snag our shirts and poke our skin, and we begin to respond in ways we don't want to.

Wisely God gave us a tool to combat the temporary blindness circumstances can impose. That tool is song. Music is a beautiful gift in and of itself. However in Scripture, song serves a deeper purpose than just personal enjoyment.

In the Bible, we repeatedly see the call to sing to the Lord—to sing His praises; to sing about His love, His faithfulness, His victory, and His strength. We are called to sing about His glorious name and His greatness, generally and specifically. Song is a form of worship,

Song as a form of worship realigns our hearts and minds with God.

and it serves a critical purpose in realigning our sight and our attitude to be more in tune with the Lord's, leaving little room for despair or anger to get toe-holds.

Music touches the depths of our emotions. It draws us nearer to the Lord as we worship with open hearts. Filling each day with songs of worship keeps our hearts and minds on the majestic and glorious, a place where, as followers of Christ, we'll be camped for all eternity.

Practice worshiping with song long enough and our lives themselves become songs of worship, giving testimony to all His wonderful works. In living this life of praise, we discover a peace that defies circumstances. What a glorious way to live!

Reflections: What hymn or Christian song has meant the most to you? Why were you so moved by it? Tap into the power of song by setting up a playlist of worship music on one of your digital devices or purchasing a new CD; make listening a daily practice.

Dear Lord, thank You for the gift of song. Thank You for giving me such a valuable tool to use in my often messy life. May my life become a song of worship to You, giving voice to Your marvelous works and bringing me a peace that defies human logic. In Jesus' name, Amen!

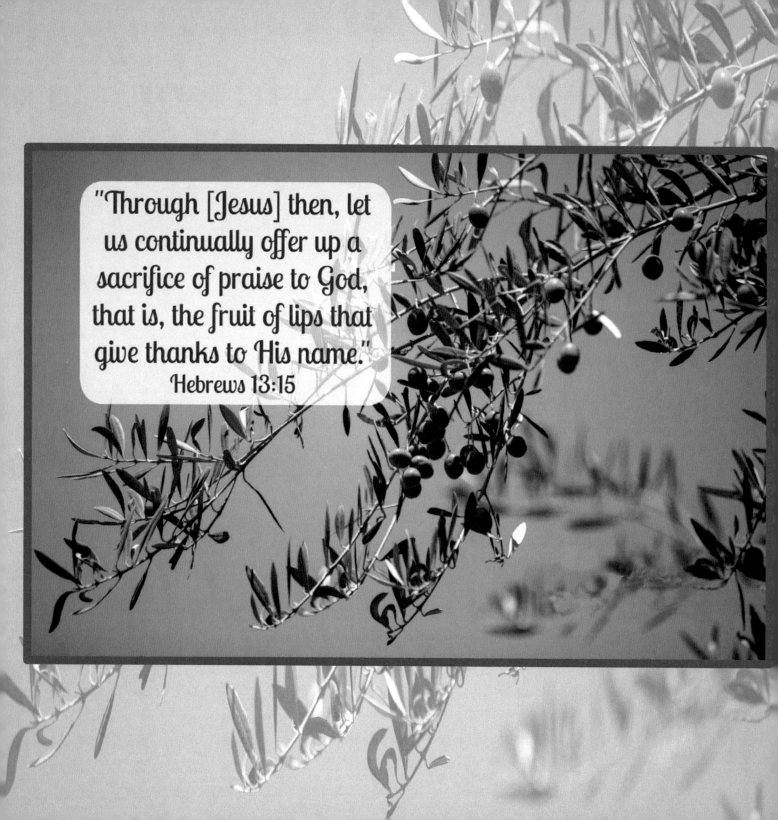

When Praising God Is Difficult

*"Through [Jesus] then, let us continually offer up a sacrifice of praise to God,
that is, the fruit of lips that give thanks to His name."*
Hebrews 13:15 NASB

It seems wrong to say, but sometimes it's not easy to praise God. The world flips upside down, fierce storms hit, the moment turns gray and ugly, day after monotonous day drags on … and praise turns hard. Worshiping God and giving Him glory becomes difficult.

But that's the point: Praise doesn't have much meaning if it's always easy. Praise itself is a form of surrender and sacrifice. We need to remember that God doesn't *need* the praise, but we *need* to give it.

Praise is the sweetener for our hearts.

In mounds of dirty dishes and days of sick kids, in financially lean months and challenging-health ones, in relational conflicts and times of isolation, praise brings perspective. A perspective we need.

Oh, God is worthy to receive our praise, absolutely! But we are also needy to *give* our praise. It's a heart thing really. Things happen and our hearts get all twisted and sour. If we're not careful, the acid oozes out, poisoning all we contact and connect with.

But by grace, we have praise. Praise is the sweetener for our hearts. It chases away the bitterness, anger, and despair of living in a world where deep, dark shadows chase us.

Praise isn't optional; it is essential for the faithful to remain faith filled. It opens our hearts to the One who can keep them soft and sweet in an often hard and bitter world. Giving thanks and praise: it's not because we always feel like it, but because we *must*.

Reflections: What difficult circumstances are you currently facing? Do you feel like praising God or not? How can praising God when you don't feel like it change your heart?

Dear Father, You are worthy of all my praise, but in the difficult times, I don't always feel like worshiping You. Help me to always offer You a sacrifice of praise, no matter how I feel, knowing that not only are You worthy, but that I need it. By Your grace and in Jesus' name, Amen!

Ascribe to the LORD the glory due his name; bring an offering and come before him. Worship the LORD in the splendor of his holiness.

1 Chronicles 16:29

Ascribe to the Lord...the Ultimate Offering

"Ascribe to the LORD the glory due his name; bring an offering and come before him. Worship the LORD in the splendor of his holiness."
1 Chronicles 16:29 NIV

It's what God asks of us: an offering, so simple yet tremendously profound: bending low to glorify Him on high. Sometimes, we believe we have nothing to give. Our offering appears so little. But giving God our full and surrendered worship is everything.

The widow did it in Mark 12:41-44. She gave a tiny amount, her last penny actually. In the splendor of His holiness, she gave it. And God set her up as the poster child for giving. So little, but such a great sacrifice, her offering seemed like pittance to all but the Lord. It truly was the greatest

> **The greatest offering is a heart sold out to God.**

offering because it came from a heart of tremendous love and devotion, from a woman who gave fully because He gave fully first.

For what else does God want but a surrendered soul, a sold-out heart, totally devoted to worshiping Him in word and deed? When we embrace His grace and power, our lives become a living example of such adoration.

Don't believe you have much to give? Through God's power and grace, our lives can become sold out, surrendered to Him in worship. That's the best offering ever! Praise the Lord on high!

Reflections: Do you worry you don't have anything of value to offer God? Have you considered that what He really wants is you; not dutiful giving, but your fully surrendered heart and soul? Don't focus on what you have to give to God. Instead, ask Him to help you live a life devoted to Him, sold out in every way. Record your prayer (or the printed one below) in your journal.

Dear Lord, You don't ask for a little from me; You ask for it all: the ultimate offering. All my devotion. All my passion. All my praise. All my worship. And You make it possible for my little to be enough. Help me to live a life sold out to You. For only You are deserving! Only You are worthy! Only You should receive my praise and glory. To You, Lord, glory forever and ever. Amen!

Why You Must Remember

*"Bless the LORD, O my soul, And all that is within me, bless His holy name.
Bless the LORD, O my soul, And forget none of His benefits."
Psalm 103:1-2 NASB*

"Bless the LORD, O my soul.!" The Lord deserves our praise, yet the messy and unexpected happenings of living in a broken and sin-filled world makes doing so difficult at times. At least it does for me. During easy and comfortable seasons, my heart sings. But when my children behave like…well…children, my wallet grows terribly thin, my husband becomes distracted, and my head aches, my heart starts muttering. My feelings begin to dictate my actions in spite of the truth.

Live anxiously, informed by circumstances, or live expectantly, informed by God's faithfulness.

I know difficult times give rise to more opportunities for growth. I know the Lord has only good plans for me. I know that even on my worst days I'm incredibly blessed. I know the Lord is working in even *this*. But my head knowledge doesn't always reach my heart. Thank God the Psalmist doesn't leave me or you stuck. He reveals the clue on how to bless the Lord in all the seasons and circumstances of our lives. We are to "…forget none of His benefits (vs. 2)."

It's really that simple. The key to everyday praise lies in remembering God's blessings. When we recall His benefits to us, we can rise above our circumstances and bless Him in the midst of the struggles. We can let the truth of what He's already done for us and His constant presence in our lives reach our hearts, transforming it to sing His praises despite what is unfolding in our lives.

Each day we have a choice: live anxiously, informed by our circumstances, or live expectantly, informed by God's faithfulness. The second brings far more joy and peace. Because life becomes an adventure when we look at its blessings and possibilities instead of its difficulties and limitations!

Reflections: How do you convince your heart to keep on praising God in unwanted circumstances? Have you adopted the practice of remembering God's faithfulness? Start journaling prayer requests, and then include the answers to those prayers as part of a faithfulness report to reflect back on.

Dear Lord, You provide me with every reason to bless You. But sometimes, it's hard. My feelings get in the way of the truth of Your faithfulness. Help me to recall Your benefits, to praise You in all my circumstances. In Jesus' name, Amen!

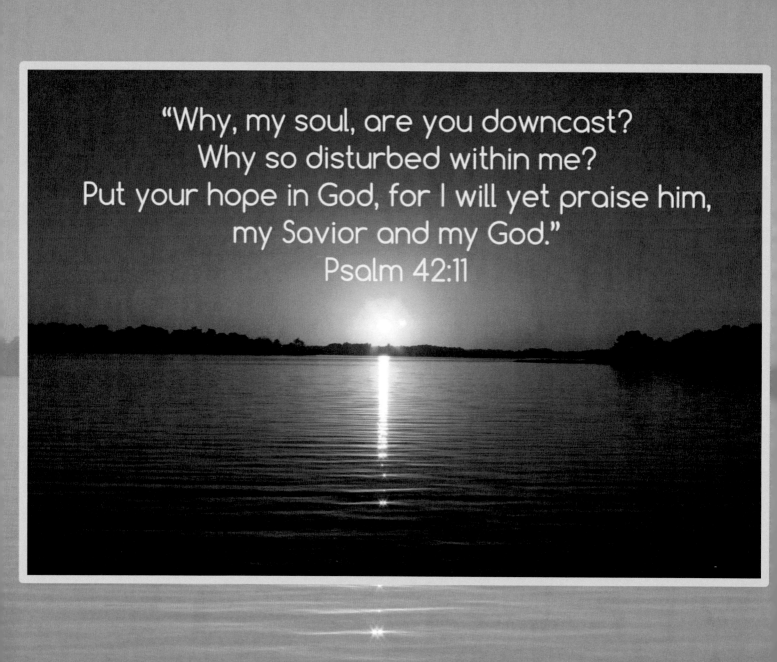

Where to Find the Security You Long For

"Why, my soul, are you downcast? Why so disturbed within me? Put your hope in God,
for I will yet praise him, my Savior and my God."
Psalm 42:11 NIV

Stumbling through the darkened woods, my soul screamed for justice and fairness. Where was God when I needed Him the most? Why would He abandon me and the tiny life that had been growing in me? Didn't He care? My tirade continued that evening until exhausted I sank to the damp coolness of earth. My heart lay in pieces. During a tumultuous decade of pregnancies and miscarriages (punctuated by four joyous live births), I never doubted God's love existed, but I did wonder whether that truth pertained to me.

> **God's sovereign will is not always what we would choose, but it doesn't change the truth of His love for us.**

Well, the Lord is full of grace, so into my life He sent a doubt-breaker, a sight-restorer by the name of Rachel. My third living child, Rachel was born with significant special needs that became apparent over several years. Yet as she grew, evidence of God's goodness began healing my self-righteous blindness.

I began to see challenges in a new way. I began to understand five principles that grounded my faith: (1) God's faithfulness does not depend on my feelings; (2) God's love is the same yesterday, today, and tomorrow; (3) God is near even when I can't feel Him; (4) God's will is always for my best, even when it doesn't feel like it; and (5) God's Word is truth whether I choose to believe it or not. You see, God's sovereign will is not always what we would choose, but it doesn't change the truth of His love for us. He loves us enough to give us what we need, not only what we want.

Reflections: Looking back on a difficult time in your life, which of the five principles did that challenge finally reveal? Which truth have you most struggled to believe? Jot down these principles on a note card or in your journal. Next time things get stormy, let His truth encourage you.

Dear God, at times my soul gets downcast. Yet You know my struggles, and You provide the strength I need to face them. Lord, remind me of the truth of Your love and faithfulness. During hard times, infuse my soul with hope as I continue to praise You in all circumstances. Resting in Your love. Amen!

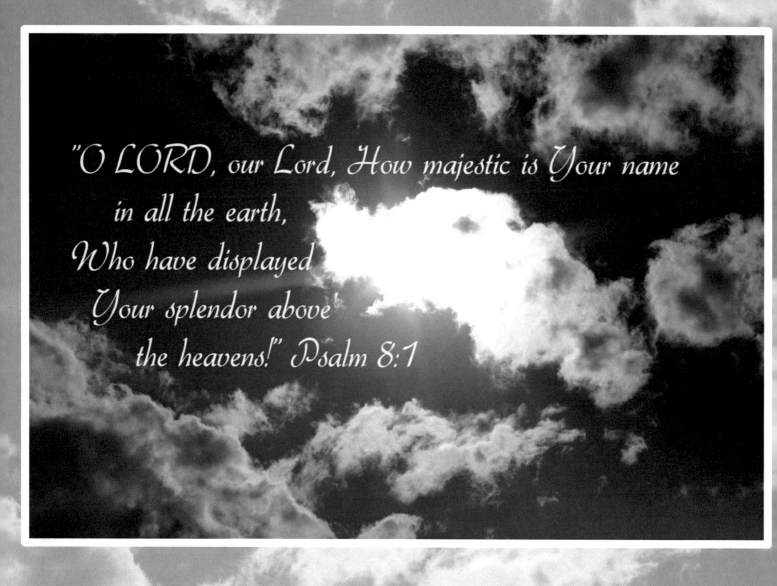

How Majestic Is Your Name!

"O LORD, our Lord, How majestic is Your name in all the earth,
Who have displayed Your splendor above the heavens!"
Psalm 8:1 NASB

In daily life, it's easy to become far-sighted, only noticing the urgent and persistent. We miss the big picture. We get so engrossed in the details of our life, we sort of set God aside. I've done it. Viewed up close, I see my life as a tangled mass of mess. Instead of an ingenious idea, it looks like an impending wreck.

But there's good news. Although we don't have the capacity to see the big picture of our lives, to see where we're going and how we will get there, God tells us He does. Moreover, He has "plans for [our] welfare, not for disaster, to give [us] a future and a hope" (Jeremiah 29:11b, HCSB).

He not only sees our lives from start to finish, but He drew up the plans…always for our good to His glory. When viewed through God's all-encompassing lens, each of our journeys showcases a masterpiece of design—lovingly and uniquely composed by the very hands of our Creator, the twists and turns adding to its beauty.

> *Our life journeys showcase a masterpiece of design—the twists and turns adding to its beauty.*

Since our sight is limited, we sometimes need to be reminded of the majestic wonder of the great I AM and His provisions for us. For me, that involves outings to remote areas where the heavens kiss the earth, where I get swallowed up in its vastness. The magnificence of such places speaks to a Greatness we cannot comprehend. It speaks to the majesty of the Creator and Sustainer of the universe and reminds us of the glorious plan He also has for each of us.

Reflections: Where have you seen the most spectacular display of the heavens? How did that experience put your life in perspective? How does such splendor showcase God's design or care for His entire creation, including each of our lives?

Dear God, the vastness of the heavens speaks to a greatness I cannot comprehend, it showcases You, Lord, the great I Am. Knowing You created a masterpiece when You designed my life helps me live with the bigger picture in mind and brings me comfort when all I can see is a tangled mess. Thank you for the glorious plan of my life. In Your Son, Amen!

"Arise, bless the LORD your God
forever and ever!
O may Your glorious name
be blessed and exalted
above all blessing and praise!"
Nehemiah 9:5b

Bless His Glorious Name!

"Arise, bless the LORD your God forever and ever!
O may Your glorious name be blessed and exalted above all blessing and praise!"
Nehemiah 9:5b NASB

Have you noticed that when winter sets in, people quit living? I don't mean only during those cold months of the calendar year. Whether walking through a season of difficult weather or difficult circumstances, people too often lose weeks and months of their life due to discontentment or despair over their situation.

Yes, life can certainly seem unwelcoming, even hostile at times. I've felt it too. But living in the midst of the cold and dreary is no reason to quit living. There is still beauty to be found. There are still things to smile about. The sun still rises each morning. There is brilliance in the setting sun and refreshment in the cool breeze. There is still so much to grab hold of and live for.

> **Peace and joy can always be found in God's poured-out blessings—grace notes that season our days.**

Life turns truly ugly only when we stop appreciating. And as hard as life can be, we always have something to appreciate. Because even in the hardest day, peace and joy (yes, even joy) can be found in God's poured-out blessings, the grace drops He delivers each day. The seemingly insignificant, often forgotten gems spawn a life worth celebrating, regardless of circumstances.

No day is perfect, but our God is, and He provides abundant blessings to remind us of that truth. All we need to do is look around and take note of the sweet and spicy the Lord sprinkles into our lives, the grace notes that season our days.

Reflections: Do you let your eyes focus on the drab and lifeless when circumstances get hard? Decide today to intentionally look for the grace notes that dot your landscape each day, and start a running list of things (big and little) for which you are grateful. Recording three a day is a great practice to develop.

Lord, thank you for seasoning my life with gems of grace. Your poured-out blessings always give me reason to live with joy and peace. Draw me into a lifestyle of praise—a habit that will help me quit focusing on my difficult circumstances and begin to appreciate the grace notes you continually season my days with. In Jesus' name, Amen!

"The LORD is my strength and my song;
He has become my salvation.
This is my God,
and I will praise Him,
my father's God,
and I will exalt Him."
Exodus 15:2

The Lord Is My Strength

"The LORD is my strength and my song; He has become my salvation.
This is my God, and I will praise Him, my father's God, and I will exalt Him."
Exodus 15:2 HCSB

Most of my life I've fought against being weak. Raised with older brothers, I grew a competitive spirit and an "I can do it" attitude. So when things spiraled out of my control as a young wife, I fought hard against the feeling of weakness ushered in by the circumstances. Yet the harder I fought, the weaker I grew.

Finally at rock bottom, I found a strength that had nothing to do with my abilities. God offered an anchor that would hold me through any storm. He gave me not only a hand up, but hope against hope for all this world would hurl my way.

> **Moments of our greatest weakness are opportunities for tapping into our greatest Strength.**

As I look back over the years I've walked with the Lord, those times of deepest sorrow have brought the greatest triumphs. Those times of utter weakness have brought greater strength. Not because I've become stronger personally through the losses and struggles, but because I've become closer to the one who is my strength—the One who has saved me.

Moments of our greatest weakness are opportunities for tapping into our greatest Strength. When we admit our weakness, we ride into battle with the One who has already secured our victory. That's all the more reason to sing His praises!

Reflections: In what area(s) of your life do you hesitate to acknowledge your weakness so you can lean into the Lord's strength? Why do you think you hold on so tightly to your perceived strength? Admit your weakness to the Lord, cloaking yourself with His strength.

Dear Father, the trials of this life seek to destroy my peace and happiness. At times, I wonder how I'll ever laugh again. Eventually the pain and sorrow drives me to my knees. And that's where I find my hope. On my knees I am forced to look up, and You are there. Always there. You wait patiently for me to give up my strength and embrace Yours, where I once again find beauty, peace, and joy. O Lord, there is no one like You. May my words and actions bless you, bringing glory daily to Your name. In Jesus' name I pray. Amen!

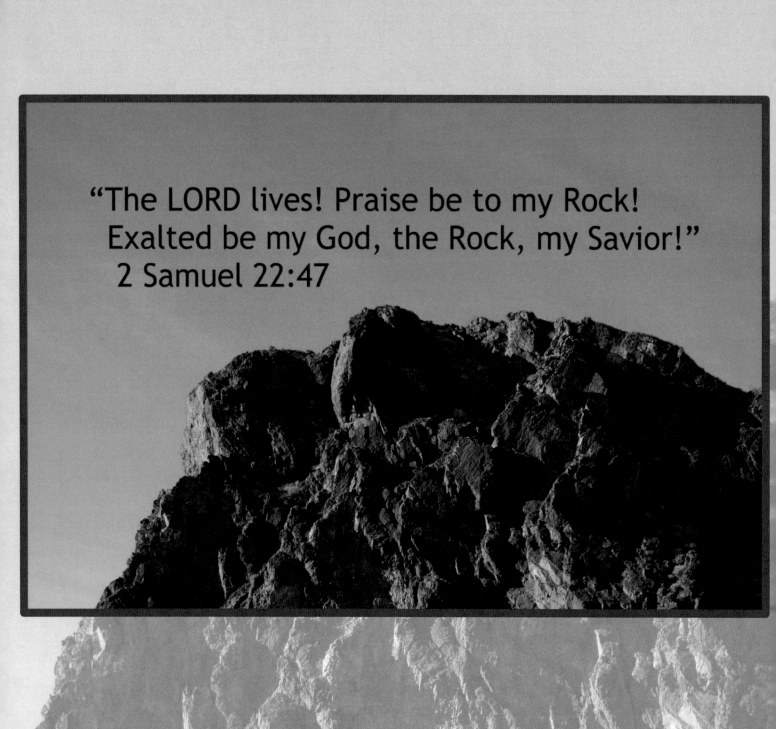

"The LORD lives! Praise be to my Rock! Exalted be my God, the Rock, my Savior!"
2 Samuel 22:47

The Lord Lives! My God, the Rock, My Savior!

"The LORD lives! Praise be to my Rock! Exalted be my God, the Rock, my Savior!"
2 Samuel 22:47 NIV

Having my children step out of the nest as young adults has proved a difficult transition for me. Not only do I miss their presence, but the daily news reminds me of the **brokenness** they're walking into. With every heartrending story, I long to pull them close, to shelter them from the evil in the world. It's tempting to give into fear. Fear of the future they face. Fear of the unknown.

Yet, I know better. An empty grave points me to faith not fear. I know the Lord lives. Because He lives, we can face tomorrow without fear. Because the Lord lives, we have the promise of life (John 14:19), a life that extends into eternity.

> **Because the Lord lives, we have the promise of life.**

We needn't fear or disdain what will come because God holds our futures in His hands. Better yet, we're never asked to enter it alone. Jesus occupies our past, walks in our present, and waits ahead in our future. It's a glorious picture of being met and kept in all our moments. Every. Last. One. The ones we lived. The ones we're living. The ones we'll soon be in. In Him all fear is wiped away.

Because Jesus lives, we can step into the future with confidence, trusting we are not stepping into a void of the great unknown, but instead into the plans of the great I AM, who was and is and is to come!

Tomorrow may never be mine or my children's, but if it is and we awake to another day, I can trust my Savior will be there to walk through it with each of us. What greater reason is there to praise the Lord!

Reflections: What tempts your heart to give into fear? What makes you lose sight of the fact that Jesus defeated death and with it any fear of what the future may hold? Write down the words from Luke 24:6, *"He is not here, but He has risen."* Reflect on them, and believe the promise of life!

Lord, because You live, I need never fear. Yet my heart still goes there at times. During those instances comfort me and remind me of Your victory. Show me, dear Jesus, the empty tomb. Help me step confidently into the plans You have for me. In Your name, I pray. Amen!

"I will proclaim the name of the LORD. Oh, praise the greatness of our God!"
Deuteronomy 32:3

Proclaim His Name!

"I will proclaim the name of the LORD. Oh, praise the greatness of our God!"
Deuteronomy 32:3 HCSB

The longer I walk with God the stronger my desire becomes to do more than thank Him or request things from Him. Although good and right aspects of prayer, they don't provide the fullness of the relationship with the Almighty I'm growing to desire.

Spending time with God and in His Word has brought me to a new level of worship. Reflecting on His goodness fills my heart with gratitude. Considering His faithfulness floods me with a sense of peace and joy. The truth of His majesty and mercy saturates my soul and fuels a desire to praise Him. More than that, it compels me to live a life of praise.

A life of praise is fueled by daily doses of Bible study, song, and thanksgiving. Such practices create an atmosphere of worship. They remind us of His love, His majesty, and His promises. They open our hearts and souls to experience His

> **Praise pours forth when we draw near to the Lord and experience His fullness.**

greatness. In the fullness this generates, praise pours forth, giving voice to the stirrings of a heart passionate for the Creator!

Despite the trials of this life—in the midst of the hardship and ugliness of this world—the Lord is worthy of all glory and honor. When we drink deep of His love and grace, it'll pour out in a life of praise.

Reflections: Time spent in the Word or in prayer often triggers feelings that beg to be expressed. Do you make it a daily practice to fill up with the fullness of the Lord? Take a few minutes to reflect on the goodness of God. As you do, let the stirrings of your soul pour forth in prayer, poem, or song of praise, a beautiful expression of worship.

Dear Lord, You grace me with Your presence and so much more. Remind me to draw near to You daily, so I can be filled. In Your fullness, my heart can't help but pour forth in praise. May I ever proclaim Your name, giving voice to the love and gratitude I feel. In Jesus' most holy name, Amen!

"Let every creature praise his holy name for ever and ever."
Psalm 145:21b

Praise His Holy Name!

"My mouth will speak in praise of the LORD. Let every creature praise his holy name for ever and ever."
Psalm 145:21 NIV

I love using pictures to focus attention on the Lord. Photographs frame the marvels of God's hand: the uniqueness, creativity, and complexity. They simultaneously display His beauty, magnificence, and tenderness.

As beings created in God's image, it's no wonder we're drawn to nature. His creation displays His attributes and spotlights His presence in our lives. As we gaze at the loveliness of a magnolia blossom or the might of the elephant, we feel closer to the Creator. As we observe the cycles of the seasons and the interactions of living things, we gain insight into the character of the Lord of the universe.

Experiencing nature in its various forms also helps us grow in understanding the many facets of worship. Each created entity was made to glorify its Maker in a uniquely designed manner. They do so in delightful vocal choruses, glorious visual displays, or fascinating mannerisms. Humans have an astonishing array of ways to offer our praise. We may speak it, sing it, pray it, write it, or display it in dance or through music or objects of worship. Our personality and environment largely determines the form our praise takes. The important thing is we do it.

We were each created to glorify our Maker in a uniquely designed manner.

In nature, God has provided us with wonderful and often spectacular reminders that we are all created to glorify Him. God is holy, worthy of all praise, forever and ever. May we each do so every day in our own unique and inspired way.

Reflections: What form does your praise most frequently take? Is it quiet prayer, loud singing, group worship, written reflection, etc.? This week, pick a new form of praise and incorporate it into your daily worship.

All creation praises Your holy name, Lord, and rightly so! Guide me to new forms of praise, praise that flows from a heart of abundance. Let me be reminded and inspired to offer You daily worship through Your ever-creative and fascinating creation. In Jesus' most precious name, Amen!

"Taste and see that the LORD is good!"

Psalm 34:8a

Taste and See the Lord's Goodness

"Taste and see that the LORD is good! Blessed is the man who takes refuge in him!"
Psalm 34:8 ESV

It's easy to walk through life missing its goodness. Life can be hard, and sometimes it seems easier to keep your eyes cast down. Or drudgery can set in when the ordinary blocks out the extraordinary that exists in each day. Either way we lose sight of the blessings in our lives.

I experience it as a work-at-home mom, becoming conditioned to the same sights, sounds, and smells. I experience it as a special needs mom, growing weary and fearful about the future for my daughter. If I don't intentionally guard against it, I find the present turns stale or the future grows scary.

Yet the Lord's goodness never wavers. It's there in the hard and the mundane. The problem isn't a lack of goodness on God's part but a skewed perspective on ours. In whatever current reality we find ourselves, we miss the abundant daily blessings, often because we expect them to look different.

> **Lift your eyes off your circumstances and onto God; see His goodness and praise will follow.**

We expect wealth, but are instead blessed with a country where we can freely worship. We expect health, but are instead gifted with abundant time to pray for ourselves and others. We expect children, but are instead given close friends or neighbors to serve.

What it takes is a shift of perspective. Abundant evidence exists of God's goodness. Right now you might not be able to see it in your life, but you can trust it's there, for God's faithfulness is never-ending. Lift your eyes off your circumstances and onto Him. See His goodness and praise will follow!

Reflections: Do you struggle with seeing the Lord's goodness when circumstances become messy? What practices can you incorporate in your days to remind yourself of the Lord's goodness and the abundant blessings in your life? Here are a few ideas: counting gifts; reciting Psalms; remembering God's character, including loving and unchanging. Chose one or two to begin with and slowly add more.

Lord, Your goodness never wavers. Yet, I sometimes miss the evidence of its presence in my life. Help me lift my eyes off my circumstances, so I can see the abundance You provide and praise Your holy name. In Jesus' name, Amen!

Look up! See the Glory of God

"The heavens declare the glory of God, and the sky proclaims the work of His hands."
Psalm 19:1 HCSB

I love observing the play of the sky. Sometimes minute-by-minute it flips design and color. Even as a child, the sky intrigued me. On car rides, I'd identify animals in the shapes of the clouds. In between putting up loads of hay in the barn, a little older version of me would rest on the lawn, mesmerized by the beauty and expanse of the heavens. Later as a mother, I often directed my children's gaze upward.

What is so captivating about the sky? To me, it's the power, limitlessness, and mystique. It may begin serene and lovely only to turn majestic and volatile the next instant. It displays the attributes and glory of God: the created sky reflecting its Creator.

> **The power, beauty, and immeasurable expanse of the heavens give voice to the glory of God.**

How sad then that city lights obscure the brilliant carpet of stars evident on moonless nights. What a shame that shows playing on TV have become more enticing than the shows playing in the heavens. What a tragedy that our desire to do things for God's glory often usurps our desire to observe God's glory.

The sky proclaims the work of His hands! Let's set aside time to be reminded of those marvelous works. The heavens declare His glory! Let's be intentional about noticing it. The power, beauty, and immeasurable expanse of the heavens give voice to the glory of God. Let's join in the chorus, glorifying Him in unison with all creation!

Reflections: When was the last time you intentionally rested in the magnificence of the sky? Schedule two dates in the next month to do just that, one during the day to lie on a grassy knoll and watch the sky dance, the other on a moonless night away from yard and street lights to take in the twinkling show of the stars. Record your thoughts as you glorify God in His greatness.

Dear God, I glory in the work of Your hands as I take in the limitless expanse of the heavens. In awe and wonder, may I join in the chorus of creation to proclaim Your great name. Guide me to set aside time to be reminded of Your marvelous deeds, your wondrous nature. In Jesus' name, Amen!

"The LORD is the everlasting God, the Creator of the ends of the earth."

Isaiah 40:28

Why You Never Need to Despair

"Have you not known? Have you not heard? The LORD is the everlasting God,
the Creator of the ends of the earth. He does not faint or grow weary;
his understanding is unsearchable."
Isaiah 40:28 ESV

At some point, we all grow weary in our days. And when life becomes burdensome, hope is easily missed.

My precious daughter has special needs. She will always be dependent on others to be safe and cared for throughout each day. Rachel recently became an adult, and with that my husband and I have to petition for and be granted guardianship of her.

We can have everlasting hope because God is everlasting.

This has stirred up all kinds of questions about her future: where she will live, what she will do, who will care for her when her dad and I are gone. During unguarded moments, my heart gives into panic as I search for the answers. When that happens, I remind myself that I have an advocate who knows all that was and is and is to come. He has a plan for Rachel's life (and mine)…and it is a good plan!

Our Creator is the Alpha and the Omega. He is the Beginning and the End. His understanding is unfathomable. He is Hope itself. We know little, we see less. He knows all, what has passed and what is to come. We can have everlasting hope because He is everlasting. There is no reason to despair, because the God of the universe is in charge. He is unchanging and all-knowing. He is faithful, loving, and sovereign. Our God is for us, and in light of His infinite knowledge, we can have peace in any circumstance.

Reflections: What allows fear to take root in your heart? What is your default reaction when it strikes? Print out the above Scripture verse on a card you can carry, or memorize it. When you begin to feel fearful, use it to remind you of God's greatness, His goodness, and His faithfulness.

Dear Father, You are the Alpha and Omega, the Beginning and the End. You know what was, what is, and what is to come. And, Lord, not only are You everlasting but your love for me is everlasting. So help me rest in Your knowledge, in Your wisdom, in Your care for me. Help me place my trust and my hope in You. In Jesus' name. Amen!

"... proclaim the praises of the One who called you out of darkness into His marvelous light." 1 Peter 2:9

Called Out of Darkness into Light

"But you are a chosen race, a royal priesthood, a holy nation, a people for His possession,
so that you may proclaim the praises of the One who called you out of darkness into His marvelous light."
1 Peter 2:9 HCSB

Trapped in the darkness of our sin, there is no hope … but God. But God! What a lovely sounding phrase; even lovelier in meaning. It conveys grace. It signifies mercy. It represents life. Without those two little words, we'd know only despair. Left to find the path of life on our own, we'd wander aimlessly. Yet God chose you and me. We belong to Him. A glorious truth!

To be honest, I haven't always lived as a child of the Most High. I don't always feel like His beloved daughter. But feelings have nothing to do with it. God declared it for all repentant believers. He sent His Son to secure it. And it's our truth to live out.

God wraps us in His cloak of righteousness and calls us into the light.

We continue to walk the hard road in this life, traveling through tunnels of temptation and sorrow from time to time. We'd be swallowed up in the darkness found there … but for the Lord. When we turn to Him, He wraps us in His cloak of righteousness and calls us into the light, His light, where darkness will be cast out for all eternity.

In His amazing grace we walk in victory. Therefore aware of our sin yet secure in our salvation, it's right to bow in repentance and humble gratitude for the Lord's compassion and mercy. Then lift your voice high and proclaim His praises for the world to hear!

Reflections: Have you ever doubted your adoption as a beloved child of God? Think of a time you questioned your worthiness to be an heir to the throne. Take a few minutes to search the Scriptures for some "But God" truths of grace and write them in your journal to refer to when doubt sets in.

Dear Father, I can hardly believe that in Your mercy and grace You've adopted me into Your family. You've made me an heir to Your kingdom. Thank you for offering Your Son to take me out of the darkness of sin into the light of His righteousness. In all humility and gratitude I give You thanks and proclaim Your praises. In Jesus' name, Amen!

Worthy
is the Lamb,
who was slain.
Revelation 5:12

Worthy Is the Lamb

*"In a loud voice they were saying: 'Worthy is the Lamb, who was slain,
to receive power and wealth and wisdom and strength and honor and glory and praise!'"*
Revelation 5:12 NIV

It's far too easy to believe the lies Satan feeds us that we aren't worthy to be forgiven, to be heirs to the heavenly kingdom. We listen to the reminders of all we've done wrong. We watch the reruns of our failures. But we have unending hope in One who is worthy for us.

Indeed, worthy is the Lamb, who was slain—slain for each of us! He didn't ask if we did enough. He didn't ask if we prayed or sacrificed enough. He knew better. Jesus knew no one would ever *be* enough, so He *became* enough for us.

> **Jesus knew no one would ever be enough, so He became enough for us.**

In the words of David, "Great is the LORD and most worthy of praise; his greatness no one can fathom" (Psalm 145:3, NIV). Indeed, no one can fathom His mighty works, the glorious splendor of His majesty, His abundant goodness and righteousness, His grace and compassion, His love and trustworthiness.

Never forget. Be reminded of His power and might and steadfastness. Never doubt. Our debt has been paid. In the death and resurrection of the Lamb, we are saved. Although we stumble, He's made a way. We have victory in Jesus Christ. In Him is our security and our future!

Reflections: Have you been listening to the lies of the enemy that you are unworthy in God's eyes? Do you struggle to believe you can be forgiven for your missteps and failures? Remind yourself of the Lord's victory over Satan. Jot down the statement below the verse above, but insert your name in place of "us." Refer to it often, glorifying and praising Jesus as you do.

Dear Jesus, I fall before You in praise. How can I express my gratitude for all You've done for me? Your sacrifice on the cross ... for me! I want to sing of Your praises forever. May I never forget to give You all the glory. Worthy are You, Lamb who was slain! I can pray this in confidence in Your always precious name, Amen!

Why Being Weak Isn't So Bad

"Praise be to the LORD, for he has heard my cry for mercy. The LORD is my strength and my shield; my heart trusts in him, and he helps me. My heart leaps for joy, and with my song I praise him."
Psalm 28:6-7 NIV

In the years following our daughter's diagnosis with a life-long disability, my husband and I exhausted all the resources at our disposal to help her succeed in life. Yet to this day she remains a toddler in a teenage body. It slowly became clear that no matter how much time, energy, and money my husband and I pour into helping Rachel, it will never be enough.

As devastating as that was to acknowledge, staring into the face of my deepest pain and acknowledging how utterly helpless I felt finally opened up a door to healing. Coming to the end of "me" woke me up to the reality of God in my life, allowing room for His power and grace to grow.

> **When we lay down the misconceptions of our own abilities, we awake to the possibilities of God.**

It's a powerful exchange. When we finally lay down the misconceptions of our own abilities, we awake to the possibilities of God. We learn that strength and hope don't come by striving and doing one more thing. They don't come from the latest medical developments or the strongest government. **Strength and hope come on our knees with heart and hands open to receive them.** They come when we willingly admit our weakness.

It's beautiful really. When you've done everything you can and finally realize it will never be enough, you're inviting God to show Himself enough. Trust me when I say He always shows up, and He's always enough!

Reflections: What stops you from admitting when you feel helpless and weary? Consider what it might mean to let God be enough for you. Record the areas in your life you are trying to control and surrender them to the Lord.

Thank you, Father, for Your undying love. May I continue to trust in You as my strength and my shield. May I awake to the realization that I'm not enough, but You always will be. As I do, may my heart leap for joy and may a song of praise flow from my lips. In Jesus' name, Amen!

"To the only God our Savior be glory, majesty, power and authority, through Jesus Christ our Lord, before all ages, now and forevermore! Amen." Jude 1:25

The Only True Form of Praise

"To the only God our Savior be glory, majesty, power and authority, through Jesus Christ our Lord,
before all ages, now and forevermore! Amen."
Jude 1:25 NIV

I love the Lord. I regularly offer Him my thanks as well as my praise. I welcome Him into my life. But am I really giving Him my all? Or like the rich young ruler (Mark 10:17-22), who couldn't bear to part with his wealth, am I holding something back? Am I giving Him glory, majesty, power, and authority in all of my life, or am I reserving some of it for myself?

I have to admit, I like a bit of power. I like to be in authority… at least a little. As I've acknowledged on more than one occasion, I like to appear strong. And I certainly like those pats on the back. I'm pretty sure I'm not the only one who wrestles with letting go of power and prestige. Yet Jude makes it clear, the Lord's dominion is

> **In living a surrendered life of praise, we receive all of God's peace and joy.**

all of the glory and power and authority and majesty. Furthermore, it's for now and forever!

God's infinite and merciful grace provides the opportunity for each of us to grow into living a surrendered life of praise. As we let the Lord fill our very being, we discover what it means to offer it all to Him. Everything! In all areas of our lives! In return, we receive all of Him. All His peace! All His joy!

Allowing the Lord complete dominion over our lives is a sacrifice asked of all of us—impossible for us but possible in Christ. It is the only true and complete form of praise, returning untold blessings. To God and only Him be all glory and majesty and power and authority, through Jesus Christ our Lord.

Reflections: Are you surrendering it all or retaining some, even just a bit of glory or power, for yourself? In what areas? Write down those areas and present them to the Lord as a sacrificial offering, like Zacchaeus (Luke 19:1-9) did with his wealth. Ask God to loosen their grip on your life.

Dear Lord, You truly are worthy of all glory, majesty, power, and authority. It's all Your dominion. Forgive me when I hold just a little back for myself. Help me release the hold they have on my life, no matter how tiny it may be. Cleanse me so I can give you complete and pure praise. In the Savior's precious name, Amen!

"LORD, Your word is forever; it is firmly fixed in heaven."

Psalm 119:89

Hope Is Found in the Steadfast Nature of God

"LORD, Your word is forever; it is firmly fixed in heaven. Your faithfulness is for all generations;
You established the earth, and it stands firm."
Psalm 119:89-90 HCSB

We live in a state park in a rural part of Iowa. For many years after we moved in, it wasn't uncommon to lose electricity in the middle of snow or rain storms. This never bothered me. Through the storm I trusted we'd be fine and that the electricity would be back on in a day or two. Past outages offered evidence of the electric company's faithfulness, so my hope was well-founded.

As we travel through life, we'll face many storms, some that will be far more disturbing and disruptive than a short power outage. Yet however hard the winds blow, however long the darkness lasts, we never have to doubt we'll make it through. God has promised to be our firm anchor in even the worst storm. He has promised to chase away the last vestiges of dark with His light.

The earth stands firm from generation to generation: evidence of God's steadfast nature.

And it's not just the promises we have to hold onto. Our well-founded hope stands firm in the Lord, because He has demonstrated His faithfulness in His care of the earth. Seasons cycle. Waters replenish the land. Trees root and grow. The earth stands firm from generation to generation, created and sustained by God's hand, evidence of His steadfast nature.

Look around at the evidence of His hand. Proof of His faithfulness. Proof that hope remains—in all of the difficult, chaotic, and scary times we may face. Yes, God is steadfast and faithful. Oh, praise His Holy name!

Reflections: What type of situations cause you to feel hopeless? Look around at the workings of earth and the intricacies of man, and write down the evidence you see of God's faithfulness. Let this evidence bring you hope in those times you find yourself giving into despair.

Dear God, the idea of Your faithfulness extended to all generations is unimaginable, yet You've promised that it is so. More than that, you've given me evidence to lean on. The earth in all its wonder. Mankind in all its intricacies. Help me to put doubt aside and hold onto the hope You offer: a hope founded in Your steadfast nature. In Jesus' name, Amen!

"how good it is to be near God!
I have made the
Sovereign LORD
my shelter,"

Psalm 73:28b

The Perfect Vantage Point from Which to Worship

*"But as for me, how good it is to be near God! I have made the Sovereign LORD my shelter,
and I will tell everyone about the wonderful things you do."*
Psalm 73:28 NLT

While on a canoe trip with my family into the wilderness of northern Minnesota, a fierce storm blew in. We braved the heavy rains until lightning forced us to seek shelter under towering pine trees. We huddled together, cold and miserable in our dripping shelter. How different it is when we let the Lord shield us! When we take refuge in Him, we may still get wet, but we no longer huddle in misery. We will still get battered by storms, but we'll be anchored firm in His harbor.

I used to find myself tossed around by my daily circumstances. I rode a roller coaster of emotions. One moment I'd be upbeat, the next would find me depressed. I grew tired of letting moment-by-moment happenings control my days. Then I discovered the blessing of reminding and remembering the greatness of God. Through a daily practice of praise and thanksgiving I became firmly anchored in Him. I now know a peace that withstands gale-force winds. Yes, life has tested it!

> Sheltered under the Lord's wings, we stand in a perfect position to give witness to all the wonderful things He has done.

Now unwanted happenings no longer hold the power they used to. Sure, I still know sorrow. I still feel regrets and heartache and anger, but they no longer rule my life, they no longer determine my joy. Snuggling near the Lord offers a new vantage point from which to view our experiences. Sheltered under His wings, we stand in a perfect position to give witness to all the wonderful things the Lord has done for and through us.

Reflections: When was a time you sought shelter from the elements of nature? How does that compare to the shelter God provides and the refuge He's offered you through the years?

Dear Lord, under Your wings is where I want to shelter. Help me to remember Your unchanging promises of grace that will anchor me in times of fierce storms. Thank you for never closing Your shelter to me. From Your refuge, may I ever give witness to Your goodness. In Jesus' name, Amen!

When You Struggle To Be Worthy in Their Eyes

"The LORD is the One who will go before you. He will be with you;
He will not leave you or forsake you. Do not be afraid or discouraged."
Deuteronomy 31:8 HCSB

We live in a world that demands proof of worth. Is it any wonder, then, that we spend so much time looking around to see who approves of us? We worry whether we'll measure up, whether our words are appropriate, whether our actions pass inspection. We walk a tightrope trying to prove ourselves and be accepted. Our flesh screams for us to measure our actions and words by what the world (or at least those in our sphere of influence) thinks.

It's frustrating how often I still fall into that trap. I look to family and friends for approval, but the Lord is the only One who perfectly loves, perfectly accepts, perfectly validates. In Christ Jesus, we have certain assurance of our worth. His death on the cross demonstrates His love for each of us.

Certain assurance of our worth exists in Jesus Christ.

So who's validation should we be looking for? It's not our neighbors', our children's, our friend's, or our spouse's. Worth in their eyes can dissipate as quickly as a wisp of smoke. We hope they care, of course. But no matter how much they love us, their acceptance is conditional, their perspective skewed.

The real validation we seek, then, should be the Lord's. In His affirmation is wrapped up all that is right and good. When we get things right with the Lord, which we do in Christ through the power of the Holy Spirit, no one else's opinion really matters. And when we fall short, which we will, He is there to remind us of His undying love and forgiveness, pouring out a grace that far exceeds our shortcomings.

God chose you, and His stamp of approval—bought with the blood of His Son—is all that matters.

Reflections: Where/from whom do you tend to seek validation? Write down all the places/people you look to for approval, then cross each one out and write "The Lord is the One" beside each as a reminder of who is the One we should look to for our worth.

Dear God, thank You for Your forever love. Thank You for Your unending grace and enduring mercy. Help me to see my worth as You do: validated in Your Son; worthy in the blood of the Lamb. May I sing Your praises, forever. Amen!

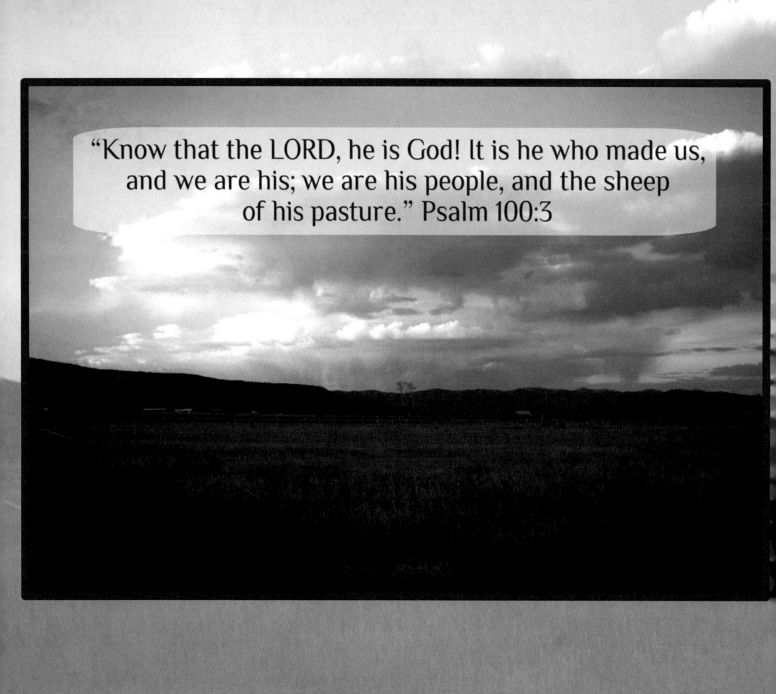

"Know that the LORD, he is God! It is he who made us, and we are his; we are his people, and the sheep of his pasture." Psalm 100:3

You Belong!

"Know that the LORD, he is God! It is he who made us, and we are his; we are his people, and the sheep of his pasture."
Psalm 100:3 ESV

Psalm 100:3 points out a sweet truth: we are the Lord's. You read it right: We belong! Best of all, we belong to the One who knows everything about each of us and still wants us as His.

If you've been a Christian long, this is not a new idea. But how many of us believe that in the deepest core of who we are? How many of us continue to doubt and question and wonder if we are lovely enough, good enough, worthy enough to be chosen by Him? Whenever I stumble in my walk with Jesus, I'm tempted to doubt. Whenever I fail to reflect Jesus well, I'm tempted to question.

God knows everything about you and still welcomes you as His beloved child, His precious lamb.

The good news is you and I can quit wondering! We can quit striving to be accepted. We are God's beloved child, His precious lambs. He's said as much many times over in Scripture. Check out these truths! Read them slowly, letting them settle deeply into your soul.

You are loved (1 John 4:10). You are accepted (Romans 15:7). You are cared for (Philippians 4:19). You belong. You are among His people. You are a sheep of His pasture (Psalm 100:3).

Believe it! When you stray, He searches for you. When you fall, He gently lifts you up. When you hunger, He feeds you. Because all shepherds care for their own…especially the great and Good Shepherd (John 10)! Know that the Lord is God. Know that the Lord is *your* God. Know that He loves, cares for, and protects you. The Bible is filled with verses declaring us as God's children. You and I need not question it any more. Instead let's join in praising His holy name!

Reflections: Why do you doubt the Good Shepherd's love for you? Dig deep, and then replace the reason you discover with scriptural truth that you are His beloved child: the above verse is a great one to begin with.

O precious Lord! May I believe that I am Your beloved child. That as my Good Shepherd You care for me, protect me, and love me. Help me to replace any doubt I have with the truth and evidence of Your devotion to me. Thank you for Your undying love for me. In Jesus' name, Amen!

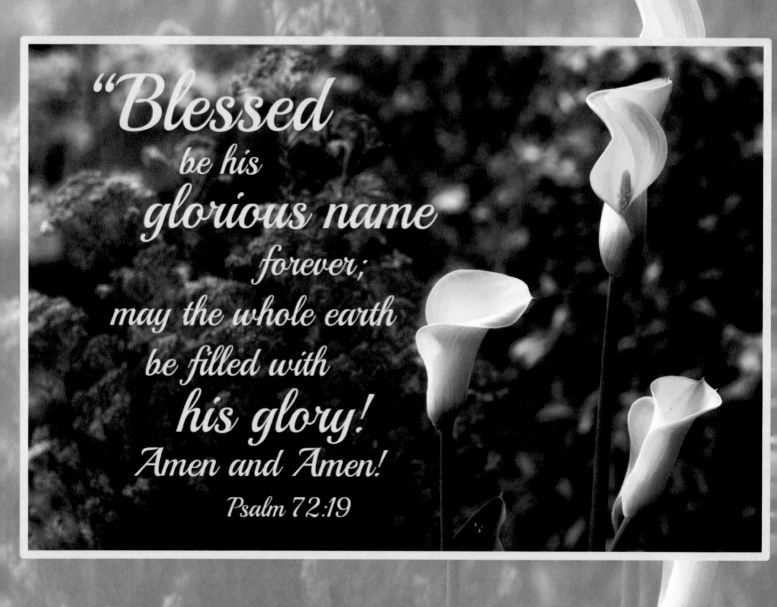

Open Your Eyes and See God's Glory

"Blessed be his glorious name forever; may the whole earth be filled with his glory! Amen and Amen!"
Psalm 72:19 ESV

God can get pushed aside in the bustle of our daily lives. His presence becomes an afterthought. His work in our lives only occasionally acknowledged. His majesty brushed aside in the pursuit of our own status. When that happens, our life becomes draped in drab hues instead of vibrant colors.

I know when my time fills beyond capacity, the beauty of my days dim as I lose sight of their Creator. It's not that the Lord's glory has diminished. Instead, our ability to experience Him in and around the happenings of our days has become compromised. The craziness and chaos of our days obscure the work of His hands and cloud the glory of His essence.

> **God's glory fills the earth, beautifying everything and infusing it all with meaning and purpose.**

The evidence of God's glory is everywhere. We only need to look around to see it. Critters, both large and small, drip with His creativity (and may I venture His humor as well). The stretching of the seasons, the slow steady rhythm of life, declares His patience. The breathless array of colors found in nature speaks to His eye for beauty. Glorious peaks, lush valleys, and eye-stretching oceans proclaim His majesty. The great expanse of the heavens and the power of the seas reveal His sovereignty.

God's glory, His presence, will always fill earth. It brightens and beautifies everything and infuses all with meaning and purpose. We simply need to push aside the blanket of busyness and apathy to notice.

Reflections: What in your life obscures your view of the great glory of God? What blinds you to His great beauty, creativity, and majesty? Write down one thing you can change in your days to better notice His spectacular and miraculous nature.

Dear God, Your glory fills the heavens and the earth, yet too often, in the hustle and bustle of my life, I miss it. I miss You! Send the Holy Spirit to stir my heart and open my eyes to Your glorious nature, Your majesty and sovereignty. Then I will be reminded to praise Your glorious name from sunup to sundown. In Jesus' name, Amen!

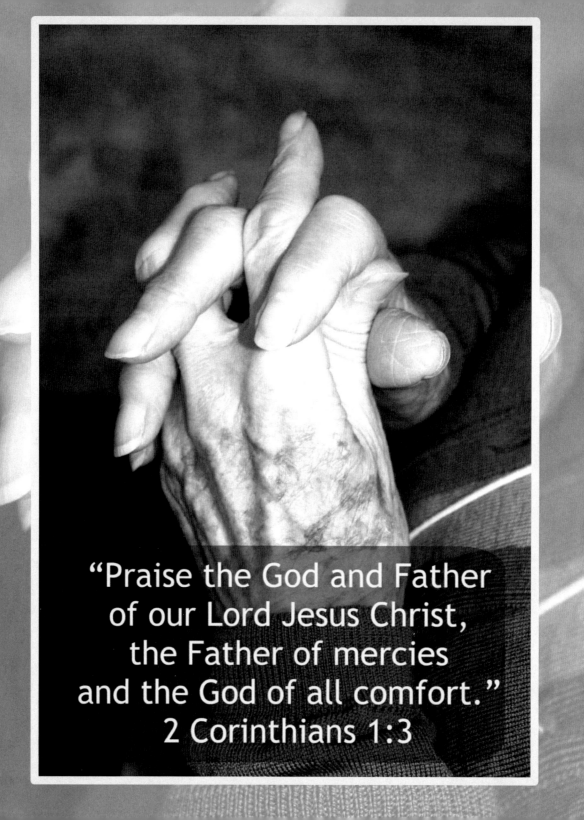

"Praise the God and Father
of our Lord Jesus Christ,
the Father of mercies
and the God of all comfort."
2 Corinthians 1:3

An Endless Well of Comfort

"Praise the God and Father of our Lord Jesus Christ, the Father of mercies and the God of all comfort."
2 Corinthians 1:3 HCSB

I was miserable, deeply depressed and believing hope had been swept out of my life. That years-ago scenario had followed the miscarriage of my first baby. Left to re-learn how to breathe again in the wake of her death, I doubted comfort was possible.

But the Lord didn't leave me there. When He knew my heart was ready, He met me in my misery, offering me a hope I had all but discounted as nonexistent.

He met me in my heartache and gave me comfort that defied the circumstances. And it didn't end there, because God doesn't only comfort us once in a while. He doesn't just comfort us when it's convenient or only in the minor aches of life. And He doesn't stockpile His hope, strength, and peace only for when the really bad hits.

> **God holds the answer to the deepest hurts of this life as well as the ongoing aches that are a part of every day.**

No. God is the author of comfort; He is the source of *any and all* comfort. We may think a drink or shopping or some other self-medication will ease our pain, but they are temporary at best. Without the Lord, there is no real and lasting comfort. He holds the answer to the deepest hurts of this life and the ongoing aches that are a part of every day.

God is faithful. You can trust Him. Today, give Him your pain, the big and the little, and praise Him for such undying mercy!

Reflections: With what are you struggling today? Where have you sought comfort? What's preventing you from going to God for relief? Stop whatever you're doing right now and turn to the Lord, offering Him your pain.

Dear Lord, this world can be terribly cruel. But You provide mercy and comfort to all who turn to You. Help my heart turn away from temporary balms to the only true comfort, which is found in Your hands. In Jesus' name, Amen!

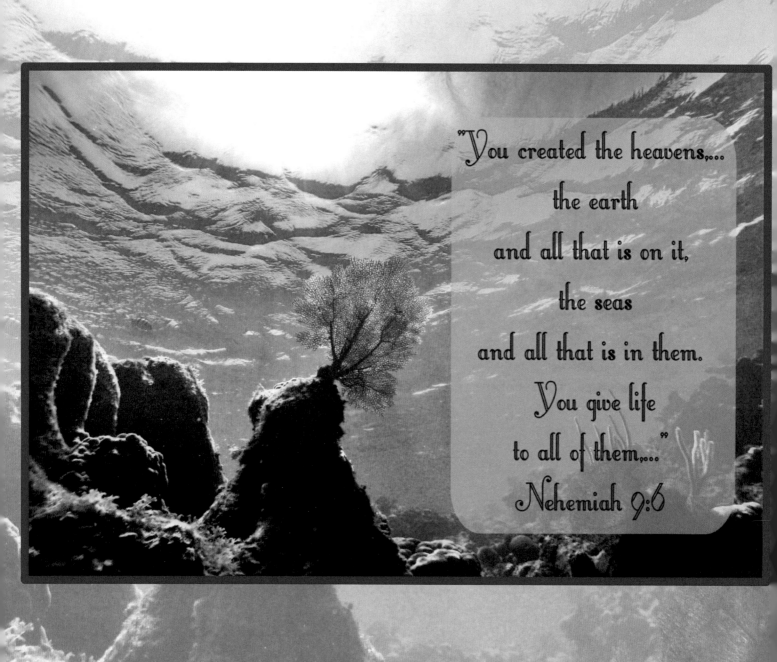

"You created the heavens,...
the earth
and all that is on it,
the seas
and all that is in them.
You give life
to all of them,..."
Nehemiah 9:6

Notice the Provider

"You alone are Yahweh. You created the heavens, the highest heavens with all their host,
the earth and all that is on it, the seas and all that is in them. You give life to all of them,
and the heavenly host worships You."
Nehemiah 9:6 HCSB

It's easy to lose sight of giving thanks or glorifying God. Distractions, busyness, struggles, illness, and weariness make it difficult to see the gift of the day and blind us to the blessings of each moment. More alarmingly, they block us from seeing the Gifter of the day.

I sensed this happening to me, this "circumstance-sightedness," and realized I needed to fight back. I needed to develop a new sense of awe, love, joy, and gratitude for the Creator of all that I am and all that I have. I needed to develop "Creator-sightedness."

> **Receive untold blessings by noticing the Provider of your life, not just the happenings, people, and things filling it up.**

This new way of seeing required more than practicing thankfulness only for what I could see. I also needed to develop an awareness of and appreciation for what was out of sight. Instead of just taking note of the happenings, people, and things in my life, I needed to notice the Provider of my life.

So I developed a daily discipline of intentionally worshiping God by (1) centering my first thought of the day on the Lord; (2) spending consistent time in God's Word; (3) jotting down and posting Scripture verses; (4) talking to God throughout the day; and (5) making a practice of listening to worship music. We won't always feel like giving thanks or glorifying God, but untold blessings are received through the consistent practice of praising the Lord as Author and Creator of all life. Simply being intentional about worship will turn circumstance-sightedness into Creator-sightedness.

Reflections: Are you intentional about noticing God in your day? Which one of the five steps listed above would add richness to your daily worship? Add it into each day this week.

Oh Father, You are worthy of all my praise. Yet the happenings in my life sometimes block me from seeing You, the Gifter of all I have and all I will receive. Help me to be intentional about developing Creator-sightedness, about becoming aware of You in my day, and about worshiping You throughout each day. In Jesus' name, Amen!

"LORD, you are my God;... you have done wonderful things, things planned long ago."

Isaiah 25:1

He Has Done Marvelous Things

"LORD, you are my God; I will exalt you and praise your name, for in perfect faithfulness
you have done wonderful things, things planned long ago."
Isaiah 25:1 NIV

Have you noticed that nothing with the Lord is accidental? What appears to be a coincidence…well…isn't. God has a plan for my life and for yours, a story that we are walking out, and He knows the details of its beginning, its middle, and its ending.

Long ago He planned your life and mine: "Your eyes have seen my unformed substance; And in Your book were all written. The days that were ordained for me, When as yet there was not one of them" (Psalm 139:16, NASB).

I find it comforting to know the Lord's hand is on every aspect of my days. It's reassuring that He knows what I need before I even need it and offers His strength before I even ask for it. Better yet, not only are we "fearfully and wonderfully made" but "Wonderful are [His] works" (Psalm 139:14, HCSB).

> **God has a plan for your life, and He knows the details of its beginning, its middle, and its ending.**

Look around you. Look closely. Look at that little one you're holding or the big one you just gave a hug to. Think about how life ends and new life begins. Indeed, think about Jesus Christ—what He has done for you. God created you to uniquely carry out the story He scripted for you. Nothing in your life is by chance. He has it all, and it's all for your good and His glory.

Think back through the years. Connect the dots. See the wonderful things the Lord has done for you and through you, and trust His plan for the future you cannot see.

Reflections: Can you see God's hand in the events of your life, a time when it seemed coincidental or accidental at first? Identify a few obvious times and a couple less obvious ones. Develop a scrapbook of God's work in and through your life by creating a timeline of the pivotal points in your life and how it has all unfolded.

Lord, You are faithful to provide for me. You've given me so much beauty and endless mercy and grace. What marvelous things You have planned for me. Help me to see Your hand in my life story. May I exalt and praise Your name for all eternity! In Jesus' name, Amen!

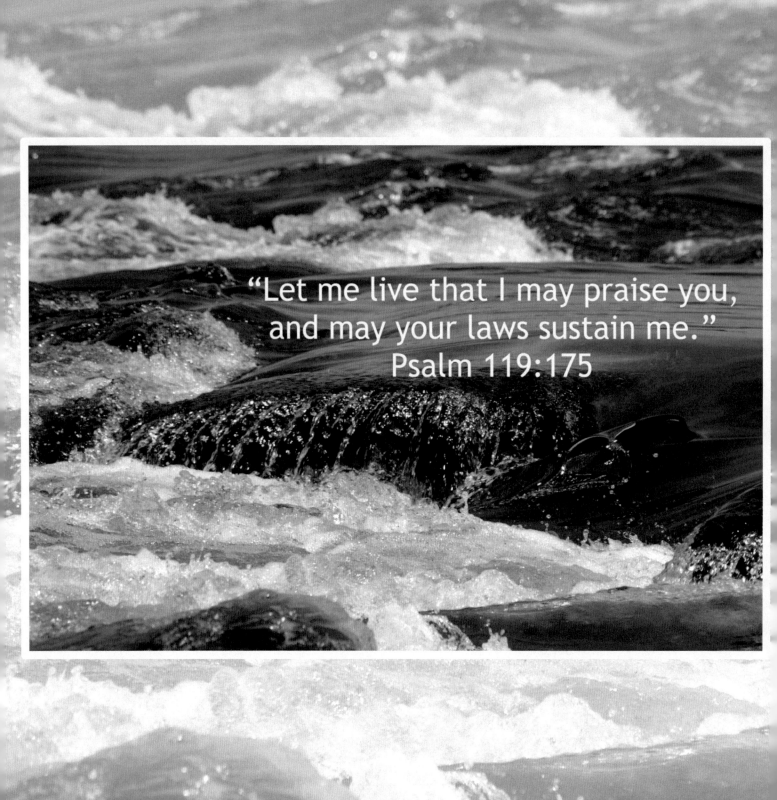

Let Me Live…

"Let me live that I may praise you, and may your laws sustain me."
Psalm 119:175 NIV

Too often we lose sight of why we're here. We look to *make something* of ourselves. We live for the fun times. We strive to make more money. We do whatever it takes simply to be happy. None of those are bad things in the proper context, but our purpose is much grander than merely satisfying our human desires. God gave us life so we can serve and glorify Him, here on earth and forever more!

God's Word rings with the freedom you long for.

We were created to praise the Maker: the One who not only created us, but sustains us, guides us, and saves us! But life distracts and pulls us away. The enemy blinds us with enticements and temptations we find hard to resist. Yet God gave us help: the Holy Bible. It took me a long time to realize the treasure that lies within those pages.

In God's Word rings the freedom we all long for. His laws guide us. His truth sustains us. His promises strengthen us. Hope, wisdom, and discernment come in the Book of Life. In Scripture, we find those words of life so painstakingly lived out before us. We discover the seeds of worship, the only fitting sacrifice for the One who offered everything for us.

In the Bible, God provides us with the source of all our praise. As we spend time soaking in His very words, we'll find them pouring back out to Him in worship, reflecting the reason for which we live!

Reflections: Are you regularly tapping into those words of life found in God's Holy Scriptures? Make it a priority to be filled up so you can pour out. Identify the best time of day for you to spend in the Word, and block it off every day on your calendar so it won't get filled by something else.

Sustain me, Lord Jesus, with Your Word, and draw me ever nearer You. Help me to be intentional about filling up with Your words of life, so I can be guided and sustained by Your truth. Because then my life can be a never-ending song of praise to You. To You be all the glory, Amen!

He is good; His faithful love endures forever.
2 Chronicles 5:13

God's Love Always Ends on the Right Petal

"…They raised their voices, accompanied by trumpets, cymbals, and musical instruments, in praise to the LORD: For He is good; His faithful love endures forever."
2 Chronicles 5:13 HCSB

Many of us run ourselves ragged chasing love. We're constantly searching, questioning, desiring. We pluck those petals and recite that childhood "love-me/love-me-not" chant[3]. We long for concrete evidence of someone's love for us.

I chased it in my younger years. At some level, I continue to do so. Perhaps we all do. But let's settle this now. It doesn't matter if you had a daddy who adored you or not. It doesn't matter if your first date turned into the "till death do us part" vow or ended in two days. It doesn't matter if you feel loved today or not. The truth is you are and always will be loved by your Father in heaven!

God's love for you is forever, whether you feel it today or not!

Why else would God send His Son to earth? Why else would He put up with our continual rejection of Him? Why else would He be infinitely patient to give us every chance to repent and turn to Him? Why else would Jesus willingly endure every manner of insult and assault; be persecuted, ridiculed, and tortured; and then allow Himself to be nailed to a cross and completely cut off from His Father? If not for love, then why?

No matter what phrase you end on with your love-me petals, know for certain God loves you! So change that chant to "love me, love me" and hand those everlasting petals of God's affection to a friend, family member, or acquaintance by sharing with them the truth of His love.

Reflections: Do you truly believe God loves you? Where else are you chasing love? Have you found what you're looking for there? Reread the Gospels to revisit the story of His love for you and then identify one person to whom you can pass on this beautiful truth.

Dear Father, thank you for your undying love for me. Help me to set down my "I love you, I love you not" petals and believe your love for me really exists forever. Guide me to pour your love out on another. In Jesus' name, Amen!

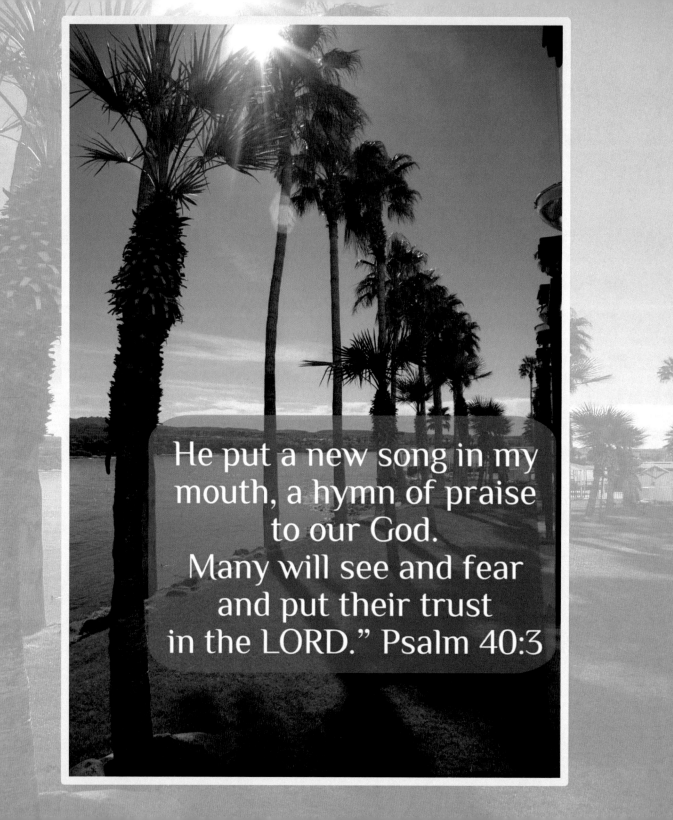

He put a new song in my mouth, a hymn of praise to our God.
Many will see and fear and put their trust in the LORD." Psalm 40:3

A Powerful Way to Witness

"He put a new song in my mouth, a hymn of praise to our God.
Many will see and fear and put their trust in the LORD."
Psalm 40:3 HCSB

Circumstances can weigh so heavy they make praising God difficult if not impossible in our own strength. I found myself burdened in that manner during the years I trudged through multiple miscarriages. I continue to have such moments as I raise my daughter who has special needs. How comforting, then, to know that when we don't have praise on our lips or songs in our hearts, God Himself will put them there. He Himself gives us a hymn of praise when we have none.

He did that for Paul and Silas after they'd been beaten and imprisoned: "About midnight Paul and Silas were praying and singing hymns to God, and the other prisoners were listening to them" (Acts 16:25, HCSB). Did you catch that later part: other prisoners were listening! They're listening to (and watching) me and you too. "Many will see and fear and put their trust in the LORD."

God Himself will give you a hymn of praise when you have none.

Nothing is easy about singing and praising God when your heart is broken and everything looks hopeless. It's near impossible really! But if it were easy, no one would notice. If it were easy, we could do it in our own strength. Instead, by the grace of God, we can do the hard job of praising Him in even the most difficult situations, bringing us a peace that passes all human understanding. Even more beautiful is that others will notice as well.

We are witnesses to the greatness of our God. So regardless of your circumstances, let a hymn of praise be always on your lips.

Reflections: Where do you look for your song of praise? Do you look to your own strength, or do you invite God to fill your heart with joyful hymns when your circumstances silence you? Identify the times you typically find yourself void of songs of praise and ask God to provide them for you.

Dear God, some days I have no words. How then can I praise You? Father, fill my heart with a song of praise, a hymn of glory that passes all human understanding, that defies the circumstances I find myself in and shines for others to see. In Jesus' precious name, Amen!

Let everything that breathes praise the LORD

Psalm 150:6

The Wellspring of Praise

"Hallelujah! Praise God in His sanctuary. Praise Him in His mighty heavens.
Praise Him for His powerful acts; praise Him for His abundant greatness.
Praise Him with trumpet blast; praise Him with harp and lyre.
Praise Him with tambourine and dance; praise Him with flute and strings.
Praise Him with resounding cymbals; praise Him with clashing cymbals.
Let everything that breathes praise the LORD. Hallelujah!"
Psalm 150 HCSB

Praising God isn't so easy when the junk of this life clings to us, weighing us down. How can we dance and sing or play the harp and tambourine when we can barely lift our heads?

We can't unless we shift our focus from us to Him! Because ascribing glory and honor to the Lord has nothing to do with our circumstances and everything to do with Him. The wellspring of authentic praise and worship doesn't come from our own strength or ability or circumstances. It bubbles up and spouts forth from the Lord Himself!

Praise in the difficult seasons of life springs forth from a wellspring God supplies deep within us.

Our joy is "in God my Savior." Our praise pours forth *in Him.* When we walk in the hope, love, and strength of the Lord, all the junk of this world sloughs off and we are free to worship with abandon.

In the joy of the Lord, all our burdens are lifted, our strength is revived, and our worship becomes deep and rich. Take your eyes off you. Place them on the source of all goodness. Let them linger on the reason we have hope. And the cymbals will resound an unceasing Amen and Hallelujah!

Reflections: In times of deep stress and distress do you focus on the circumstances, or do you turn to God and draw from His wellspring of praise? Psalm 119 is filled with words of delight for God's Word. Spend time this week identifying and recording passages of this beautiful psalm that fills your soul with praise.

God of all power and might, Your abundant greatness I cannot fathom. Your mighty acts are too vast for me to comprehend. Give me a heart of worship, Lord, so I can praise You as long as I have breath. Hallelujah, Amen!

Let's Journey Together Toward Greater Peace

Despite the trials of this life…in the midst of the hardships, in the ugliness of this world, the Lord is worthy of our praise. God created us to be in relationship with Him.

And then sin happened. Our fellowship with the Father broken, we wandered through life lost.

But then God! He sent His one and only Son that whoever should believe in Him would be saved!

The chasm bridged. The relationship restored.

No wonder we thrive in worship! No wonder praise brings about restoration of the soul! Our souls long to be walking in the "garden" with our Creator. But until Jesus returns again to establish heaven on earth, the closest thing to that walk in this life is found during worship.

> *Spending time with God and in His Word fuels a desire to praise Him.*

As we draw nearer to God in praise, prayer, and community and personal study, we'll rediscover the beauty of walking with our Lord. As we glorify Him, we'll find a peace that transcends the hard and mundane. As we learn to embrace Him before, after, and in the midst of each day, we'll find a joy that defies the circumstances.

May we each continue to sing and praise the Lord in all circumstances. May our constant worship bring glory to God and draw others to Him.

I'm praying for you on this journey.

Download Your Free Companion Journal

To help you get the most out of this devotional, I've created the *Everyday Praise Companion Journal*. You can print this PDF document out and use it to record your thoughts and reflections. This is my free gift to you.

Simply download it to your device, print it out, bind it however you want, and enjoy! If you have your own journal you want to use, go right ahead. However, feel free to download this one too. The important thing is to take time to journal your praise journey. It'll remind you of where you started and give you a glimpse to where God is taking you.

Visit www.juliesunne.com/everydaypraisedevotional to request your free *Everyday Praise Companion Journal*.

"As a child of God, our whole reason for existing is to give God praise. What a testimony to give in a difficult situation."

—Monica Johnson

Points to Remember

Praising God is the way over any mountain, through any swamp, and across any valley.

Praise settles souls and ushers in lasting peace.

Song as a form of worship realigns our hearts and minds with God.

Praise is the sweetener for our hearts.

The greatest offering is a heart sold out to God.

Live anxiously, informed by circumstances, or live expectantly, informed by God's faithfulness.

God's sovereign will is not always what we would choose, but it doesn't change the truth of His love for us.

Our life journeys showcase a masterpiece of design—the twists and turns adding to its beauty.

Moments of our greatest weakness are opportunities for tapping into our greatest Strength.

Peace and joy can always be found in God's poured-out blessings—grace notes that season our days.

Because the Lord lives, we have the promise of life.

Praise pours forth when we draw near to the Lord and experience His fullness.

We were each created to glorify our Maker in a uniquely designed manner.

Lift your eyes off your circumstances and onto God; see His goodness and praise will follow.

The power, beauty, and immeasurable expanse of the heavens give voice to the glory of God.

We can have everlasting hope because God is everlasting.

God wraps us in His cloak of righteousness and calls us into the light.

When we lay down the misconceptions of our own abilities, we awake to the possibilities of God.

Jesus knew no one would ever be enough, so He became enough for us.

In living a surrendered life of praise, we receive all of God's peace and joy.

The earth stands firm from generation to generation: evidence of God's steadfast nature.

Certain assurance of our worth exists in Jesus Christ.

Sheltered under the Lord's wings, we stand in a perfect position to give witness to all the wonderful things He has done.

God knows everything about you and still welcomes you as His beloved child, His precious lamb.

God's glory fills the earth, beautifying everything and infusing it all with meaning and purpose.

God holds the answer to the deepest hurts of this life as well as the ongoing aches that are a part of every day.

God's love for you is forever, whether you feel it today or not.

Receive untold blessings by noticing the Provider of your life, not just the happenings, people, and things filling it up.

God has a plan for your life, and He knows the details of its beginning, its middle, and its ending.

God's Word rings with the freedom you long for.

God Himself will give you a hymn of praise when you have none.

Praise in the difficult seasons of life springs forth from a wellspring God supplies deep within us.

Spending time with God and in His Word fuels a desire to praise Him.

"Whatever good we accomplish, the Lord is ultimately responsible, and He alone deserves the praise. The whole purpose of our lives is to magnify His fame and "sing the glory of his name."
— Liz Curtis Higgs, *It's Good to Be Queen*

Additional Praise Bible Verses

Growing up, I believed worshiping God happened only inside the four walls of a church building. That couldn't be further from the truth! Being a relational Father, the Lord allows direct access to him anytime and anywhere from every one of His children.

The verses I chose to accompany the devotions in this book comprise only a few of those many praise and worship scriptures that fill the Holy Bible. This section includes many more that will infuse your soul and stir your heart to pour forth praise. (All Bible verses in this section are taken from the HCSB version.)

———

"Lord, who is like You among the gods? Who is like You, glorious in holiness, revered with praises, performing wonders?"
Exodus 15:11

"He is your praise and He is your God, who has done for you these great and awesome works your eyes have seen."
Deuteronomy 10:21

"Naked I came from my mother's womb, and naked I will leave this life. The Lord gives, and the Lord takes away. Praise the name of Yahweh."
Job 1:21

"Be exalted, Lord, in Your strength; we will sing and praise
Your might."
Psalm 21:13

"Rejoice in the Lord, you righteous ones; praise from the upright
is beautiful."
Psalm 33:1

"I will praise the Lord at all times; His praise will always be on
my lips. I will boast in the Lord; the humble will hear
and be glad."
Psalm 34:1-2

"Take delight in the Lord, and He will give you your
heart's desires."
Psalm 37:4

"Why am I so depressed? Why this turmoil within me? Put your
hope in God, for I will still praise Him, my
Savior and my God."
Psalm 42:5

*"So I will praise You as long as I live; at Your name,
I will lift up my hands."*
Psalm 63:4

*"I will make known the Lord's faithful love and the Lord's praise-
worthy acts, because of all the Lord has done for us — even the
many good things He has done for the house of Israel and has
done for them based on His compassion and the abundance
of His faithful love."*
Psalm 63:7

*"May God be praised! He has not turned away my prayer or
turned His faithful love from me."*
Psalm 66:20

*"Sing to God! Sing praises to His name. Exalt Him who rides on
the clouds — His name is Yahweh —
and rejoice before Him."*
Psalm 68:4

"May the Lord be praised! Day after day He bears our burdens; God is our salvation. Selah"
Psalm 68:19

"How happy are those who reside in Your house, who praise You continually. Selah"
Psalm 84:4

"Lord, the heavens praise Your wonders – Your faithfulness also – in the assembly of the holy ones."
Psalm 89:5

"It is good to praise Yahweh, to sing praise to Your name, Most High, to declare Your faithful love in the morning and Your faithfulness at night, with a ten-stringed harp and the music of a lyre."
Psalm 92:1-3

"Sing a new song to the Lord, for He has performed wonders; His right hand and holy arm have won Him victory."
Psalm 98:1

"My soul, praise Yahweh! Lord my God, You are very great; You are clothed with majesty and splendor."
Psalm 104:1

"Praise Yahweh, for Yahweh is good; sing praise to His name, for it is delightful."
Psalm 135:3

"Heal me, Lord, and I will be healed; save me, and I will be saved, for You are my praise."
Jeremiah 17:14

"Sing to the Lord! Praise the Lord, for He rescues the life of the needy from the hand of evil people."
Jeremiah 20:13

"May the name of God be praised forever and ever, for wisdom and power belong to Him."
Daniel 2:20

"God comes from Teman, the Holy One from Mount Paran.
Selah His splendor covers the heavens, and the
earth is full of His praise."
Habakkuk 3:3

"And Mary said: My soul proclaims the greatness of the Lord,
and my spirit has rejoiced in God my Savior,"
Luke 1:46-47

"Oh, the depth of the riches both of the wisdom and the
knowledge of God! How unsearchable His judgments and
untraceable His ways!"
Romans 11:33

"For it is written: As I live, says the Lord, every knee will bow to
Me, and every tongue will give praise to God."
Romans 14:11

"Praise the God and Father of our Lord Jesus Christ, the Father
of mercies and the God of all comfort. He comforts us in all our
affliction, so that we may be able to comfort those who are in any

kind of affliction, through the comfort we ourselves
receive from God."
2 Corinthians 1:3-4

"For every one of God's promises is "Yes" in Him. Therefore, the
"Amen" is also spoken through Him by us for God's glory."
2 Corinthians 1:20

"Praise the God and Father of our Lord Jesus Christ, who has
blessed us in Christ with every spiritual blessing in the heavens."
Ephesians 1:3

"Praise the God and Father of our Lord Jesus Christ. According
to His great mercy, He has given us a new birth into a living
hope through the resurrection of Jesus Christ from the dead."
1 Peter 1:3

"A voice came from the throne, saying: Praise our God, all His
slaves, who fear Him, both small and great!"
Revelation 19:5

Endnotes

1. Thomas Ken, "Doxology," 1674. The lyrics, sung as the Doxology in many churches, are actually the last verse of a longer hymn, "Awake, My Soul, and with the Sun."
2. "It Is Well With My Soul" Words: Horatio G. Spafford, 1873. Music: Ville du Havre, Philip P. Bliss, 1876.
3. Clara Hätzlerin, The Daisy Oracle (He Loves me, He Loves Me Not), 1471, first printing, *Liederhandschrift* songbook.

Lyrics to the Referenced Hymns

Doxology

Praise God, from Whom all blessings flow;
Praise Him, all creatures here below;
Praise Him above, ye heavenly host;
Praise Father, Son, and Holy Ghost.

*Thomas Ken, 1674, Public Domain

It Is Well With My Soul

When peace, like a river, attendeth my way,
When sorrows like sea billows roll;
Whatever my lot, Thou hast taught me to say,
It is well, it is well with my soul.

Refrain: It is well with my soul,
It is well, it is well with my soul.

Though Satan should buffet, though trials should come,
Let this blest assurance control,
That Christ hath regarded my helpless estate,
And hath shed His own blood for my soul.

My sin—oh, the bliss of this glorious thought!—
My sin, not in part but the whole,
Is nailed to the cross, and I bear it no more,
Praise the Lord, praise the Lord, O my soul!

For me, be it Christ, be it Christ hence to live:
If Jordan above me shall roll,
No pang shall be mine, for in death as in life
Thou wilt whisper Thy peace to my soul.

But, Lord, 'tis for Thee, for Thy coming we wait,
The sky, not the grave, is our goal;
Oh, trump of the angel! Oh, voice of the Lord!
Blessed hope, blessed rest of my soul!

And Lord, haste the day when the faith shall be sight,
The clouds be rolled back as a scroll;
The trump shall resound, and the Lord shall descend,
Even so, it is well with my soul.

* Horatio G. Spafford, 1873, Public Domain

Acknowledgments

I know I'll miss many people who have been instrumental in getting this book published, but here's my best stab at it.

First to my Lord and Savior: Without You, there'd be no reason for this devotional. Through Your faithful love, You've transformed a frustrated, confused, and yes, angry young wife and mother into a more mature woman who is growing in her faith and deeply grateful for her many blessings. The hope You offer makes living in this fractured world not only doable but beautiful. Thank you for your undying love, unchanging truth, and unfathomable grace. May You be ever praised!

To my family, Dave, Daniel, Zachary, Rachel, and Joseph: I love you more than I can ever express. Thank you for loving me at my worst and for supporting me through the long hours of writing and publishing this book.

To Mom and Dad: I knew love from the beginning and learned how to work and play hard. I'm so grateful. I love you!

To Ruth: Thank you for letting me marry your baby, for being such an incredible model of a faith-filled woman, and for welcoming me so completely into your family. A girl couldn't have a better mother-in-law.

To my many siblings and siblings-in-law: I'm incredibly grateful for the close relationships we have. I know I can turn to any one of you during a time of need. Thank you for your love and support.

To my launch team who is willing to help a beleaguered author get the word out about this labor of love: Thank you for believing in this book and in me. I treasure your help and especially your prayers for this devotional to get into the hands God intends it for.

To my Target Mastermind colleagues and friends (Marisa, Derek, Dale, Bill, Jason, Lara, Jamey, and Mike): I would have never gotten this far without your advice, encouragement, and prayers. Thank you; you're the best!

Finally, to all who prayed and provided feedback on the project early on, and especially to Daniel, Mom, and Sherri, who were willing to be the extra eyes I needed to publish a quality devotional: You've given me the confidence to actually push the "Publish" button. Thank you!

Share the journey with me,

visit juliesunne.com

About the Author

Julie Sunne (pronounced Sun-E) balances work as a writer and editor with caring for her family of six, which includes two young adults and two teenagers. Her life has been complicated by difficult circumstances, including multiple miscarriages and a daughter with significant global disabilities. Yet as she learns to let God fill her, she is discovering that messy can also be glorious.

Julie lives with her husband David and two of their four children in a state park in northern Iowa, where her free time is filled with family, gardening, hiking, and reading. She enjoys few things more than helping women discover peace and joy in the midst of their life's messes.

Julie would love to connect with you. Choose your favorite way:

Website: juliesunne.com
Twitter: twitter.com/JulieSunne1
Facebook: facebook.com/JulieSunne1
Instagram: http://instagram.com/juliesunne1/
Pinterest: https://www.pinterest.com/juliesunne/

Made in the USA
Monee, IL
08 November 2022

17340963R00062